*In Grand Style*

To Bill, my very own capriccio, who ever enchants me.

To Joe Volpe, the grand and glorious fox,
with love, respect, and admiration.

And to the memory of Mack Harrell, my cousin,
Metropolitan Opera baritone of profound lyrical beauty,
who took me to my first operas when I was a little girl.

— NANCY ELLISON

# In Grand Style

## THE GLORY OF THE METROPOLITAN OPERA

### NANCY ELLISON

*with* JOSEPH VOLPE, JAMES LEVINE, JOSEPH CLARK *and* LUCIANO PAVAROTTI

RIZZOLI
NEW YORK

*Any artist who meets The Met will be very happy.*
*I certainly fell in love with the theater all those years ago . . .*

*This house is my true American home, and my colleagues over the years — the management and the backstage, technical, and administrative people — filled the house with a unique friendship and professionalism, and I regard them all as my New York family.*

*To head up The Met is a very privileged position, and in Joe Volpe and James Levine, two rare and special people, I have made lifelong friends and will be forever thankful for our collaboration and our beautiful time spent together.*

LUCIANO PAVAROTTI

# The Operas

7 FOREWORD
JOSEPH VOLPE

11 THE METROPOLITAN OPERA
JAMES LEVINE

13 MILITARY MANEUVERS, OR,
GETTING GRAND OPERA
ON STAGE
JOSEPH CLARK

17 GRAND AND GLORIOUS
NANCY ELLISON

24 DER ROSENKAVALIER
38 LA CLEMENZA DI TITO
48 DIE ZAUBERFLÖTE
60 AIDA
66 PAGLIACCI
76 NABUCCO
86 CYRANO DE BERGERAC
102 LA BOHÈME
110 SAMSON ET DALILA
126 I VESPRI SICILIANI
134 CARMEN
142 LE NOZZE DI FIGARO
156 OTELLO
166 TANNHÄUSER
178 RODELINDA
188 SALOME
196 UN BALLO IN MASCHERA
204 FAUST
218 TURANDOT
230 TOSCA

# Foreword

JOSEPH VOLPE

The glory of The Met! What memories, images, and dreams that phrase conjures up. For some, it evokes thoughts of past performances that live forever in the mind's eye. For others not fortunate enough to have experienced the magic of a live Metropolitan Opera performance, the glory resounds in the imagination, elicited from a recording, a telecast, or best of all, a live radio broadcast, which by its very nature stimulates the listener's own creativity and draws him or her into the creative process. And for those who have never known the joy of opera, it is my fondest hope that the volume you now hold will encourage you to open new doors in your life and enter the unique world of grand opera.

The magical transformation that takes place on the Met stage each season, seven times a week for more than thirty weeks, is a glory unto itself. No other major company even attempts such a schedule; who in their right mind would dare to undertake such a daunting challenge? I admit it takes a certain mentality. No less an eminent opera personality than the Austrian conductor Franz Schalk—who conducted in Vienna during the Gustav Mahler years, led the first uncut *Ring* cycles at The Met, and thus knew a few things about this incredible art form—said of it: "The theater is an insane asylum, and the opera house is the ward for the incurables." Incurables, indeed, but what a sublime madness it is, and what rewards we reap.

The Met's active repertory comprises more than one hundred different operas, with a range of musical history encompassing nearly three hundred years—from George Frideric Handel's *Rodelinda* to a Met-commissioned world premiere in 2005–06 of American composer Tobias Picker's *An American Tragedy*, based on the classic novel by Theodore Dreiser. Of these, we usually present twenty-eight to thirty over the course of our thirty-five-week season, with four or five of them typically new productions, and often including a world or Met premiere.

This complexity is magnified by the varied and disparate production styles of the repertory, ranging from the stage-filling, magnificent royal throne room of *Turandot's* legendary Chinese palace to the intimate garret of the poverty-stricken poets, painters, and musicians of *La Bohème*. Whatever the particular production style, it is part of what I like to characterize as the "grand style" of this book's title, for to me "grand" refers to the appeal to the full range of human emotions on the elevated scale that only opera can offer.

Of course had this book been conceived one hundred, or even fifty, years ago, "grand style" would have taken on a completely different connotation. In the first half of The Met's existence, grand style was more apt as a description of the audience rather than the stage. Indeed it is not stretching the point to say The Met itself was created purely because there was not enough grand style to go around—that it was the right company formed for the wrong reason.

By the mid-1870s, the center of New York City's operatic and social life had gravitated from Park Row north to the Academy of Music at Fourteenth Street and Irving Place. That theater was notable for its small number of boxes, the primary function of which was to act as a showplace for the brightest lights of New York society to see and be seen. But the limited number of boxes also served another purpose—to restrict membership only to the upper crust of that society, the so-called "old money."

The latter part of the century had witnessed the rise of the "new money" crowd, the masters of the universe of the time: industrialists and railroad magnates, who were later dubbed the robber barons. Scorned by the old society crowd, they were unable to obtain boxes at the Academy. What to do? Since hell hath no fury like a would-be social climber scorned—especially the *wife* of a would-be social climber—the "new money" crowd decided to take matters into their own hands. In 1880, spurred on by the wife of Cornelius Vanderbilt (of the New York Central Railroad fortune), they began an effort to build their own opera house, and in 1883 The Metropolitan Opera was born on Broadway between Thirty-ninth and Fortieth

streets—what Edith Wharton in *The Age of Innocence* referred to as the "remote metropolitan distances above the forties."

Of course, the primary requirement for the opera house was that it have enough boxes, which were arrayed in a golden horseshoe configuration, the better to display the society crowd who felt that *they* were the true stars of the theater. Oh, and by the way, an opera company was also to be created.

Since its opening on October 22, 1883, with a performance of *Faust* starring the world-renowned Christine Nilsson, The Met has been home to the world's greatest artists. But though the company presented a galaxy of stars during those formative years, most brilliantly the seventeen-year reign of Enrico Caruso and such conductors as Arturo Toscanini and Gustav Mahler, the opera's grand style still was to be found more in the auditorium than on the stage.

The physical productions were undistinguished with some exceptions, among them those by noted stage designer Joseph Urban. Often they consisted of simply painted and wrinkled flats that were interchangeable among different operas. Stage direction, if it existed at all, was minimal. The most commented-upon costumes were those worn by the box holders, not by the performing artists, with the exception of those of the few divas who brought their own costumes from Europe.

With the arrival of Rudolf Bing in 1950, the stage finally began to reflect the idea that opera was *theater* as well as music. Bing brought in directors and designers not just from the opera world, but from theater and film as well (Margaret Webster, Tyrone Guthrie, Garson Kanin, Peter Brook, Alfred Lunt, Boris Aronson, and Günther Rennert, to name a few) to revolutionize what New Yorkers were to see on the operatic stage, and in the process create what opera was meant to be—true music theater.

However, something was still missing on the musical side. Great singers have always been the hallmark of The Metropolitan Opera, as well as world-renowned conductors, nearly all of whom have graced the Met's orchestra pit. But the Met's superior musical forces, the orchestra and chorus, lacked the direction necessary to attain a consistent level. Other than the brief tenure of Rafael Kubelik in the early 1970s, The Met never had a true music director, one whose sole responsibility was to lend his full attention and talents to lead it to the musical heights worthy of The Metropolitan Opera. Toscanini served unofficially in such a role, but only for a very short time.

Enter James Levine. For more than thirty years, his talents, unflagging leadership, and commitment of time to the Met company, literally unprecedented in this modern era of jet-setting conductors, has brought our musical forces to a new level of excellence.

Thus, what we have witnessed over 120 years is a complete evolution of opera at The Met. From little more than a sideshow to showcase the stature and visibility of the New York social elite, it has become a vibrant and vital company, capable of presenting at the highest level a transforming art form that can speak to anyone who chooses to give it a chance. Refuting Samuel Johnson's description of opera as that "exotick [sic] and irrational entertainment," the eminent critic George Steiner described it as "that most extravagant of human necessities." Necessity, indeed.

So the critical elements are in place. But is that in itself enough for excellence? Not necessarily. It falls to the general manager to provide the resources and, most importantly, create the atmosphere for the thousands of dedicated and talented artists who *are* The Metropolitan Opera to perform to their utmost, to strive to reach that level of transcendence that is the unique provenance of "grand" opera. That is the role I now play. Whether that level is reached is not for me to say, but for others to decide. In the sixteen years that it has been my honor to serve as general manager, it has been my mission to do everything I can to achieve that goal, to search out the best artists the world has to offer, to bring them to our company, and to give them the freedom to do nothing less than reach for the stars.

I have always believed one of the great barriers to the accessibility of opera is language. As Edith Wharton, again in *The Age of Innocence*, wrote: "An unalterable and unquestioned law of the musical world required that the German text of French operas sung by Swedish artists should be translated into Italian for the clearer understanding of English-speaking audiences." She was exaggerating, of course, but accessibility has always been a problem. I believe we have found a solution. What I have observed with the Met Titles system is how audiences sit in rapt attention at works that in the past might have engendered only boredom and frustration, ultimately driving them away. While intuitively one would think quiet is not a desired sound at any theatrical performance, the quiet of Met audiences as they become deeply involved in the performances is deafening in its significance. Their willingness to take a chance on the unknown has allowed us to enlarge the repertory successfully with such heretofore underappreciated masterpieces as *Dialogues des Carmélites*, *The Rake's Progress*, *Wozzeck*, *Lady Macbeth of Mtsensk*, *Pelléas et Mélisande*, *War and Peace*, and many others. This has served to revitalize both the repertory and the audience, and there is no greater gauge of artistic health than that.

Only the transformative medium of great and truly epic art has the kind of vitality that can penetrate the human consciousness and raise the spirit to emotional heights. This is the true glory and grand style of The Met.

Live opera by its very nature is evanescent. It exists for but a brief moment. How do you capture it, retain and represent it in a medium that is not its own? Through a creative artist who is every bit the equal in her realm as The Metropolitan Opera company is in its. Nancy Ellison is such an artist. She brings to this project her own history as a performer and, more critically, an eye for the essence of the art of performance, for the art of capturing that fleeting moment of heightened emotion is a rare one. To call her work mere photography is insufficient. A photograph is no more than a picture, but Nancy's painterly approach enhances the image and illustrates not merely the surface, but the emotion, the mood, the play of light and color — in short, the drama. She puts you not simply on the stage, but in the hearts and minds of the characters. This is the difference between photography and artistry, and she has mastered it.

It is my fondest hope that her incredible artistry will work its magic on you as it opens up the true glory of The Metropolitan Opera, whether it revives in you that unique high you experienced at a live performance, or provides the spark that encourages you to come to The Met and embark on a grand journey like none you have ever taken.

# The Metropolitan Opera

JAMES LEVINE

Where I have made my artistic home for an unbelievable thirty-five years!

•

The largest collection of dedicated operatic artists under one roof in the world!

•

My responsibility and my inspiration have been to continue to develop our company—orchestra, chorus, and ensemble—to an ever-higher standard of artistic quality. We have been doing that together through the study and re-study, and rehearsal of more than eighty masterpieces of operatic literature and well over two thousand performances at The Metropolitan Opera House, as well as the great works of symphonic and chamber music in our annual series of concerts at Carnegie Hall.

•

Since 1980, when we founded what is now known as the Lindemann Young Artist Development Program, some of our most important and rewarding work has been the training of an extraordinary group of operatic artists of the future. Nearly one hundred graduates of this program have been or are currently working in professional companies worldwide.

•

Since 1977, when we began adding to our legacy of radio broadcasts with live televised performances, a large and eager audience that could rarely, if ever, get to a live performance could hear and see The Metropolitan Opera on TV just by pressing a button! Astounding! The very first telecast, *La Bohème*, was seen by more people that night than had attended all the performances of *Bohème* given worldwide since the work was premiered in 1896! To date, there have been over one hundred performances telecast from The Met. For us, television has been, among so many other things, a great tool for self-improvement.

•

Our repertoire has grown to the point that we can present a wide spectrum of operas of every kind. Besides the masterpieces of Verdi, Wagner, Mozart, Strauss, and Puccini and the greatest works of Bizet, Tchaikovsky, Gounod, Massenet, Offenbach, Beethoven, Giordano, Donizetti, Bellini, and Rossini, et al., now we can also offer Handel, Berg, Schoenberg, Britten, Bartók, Janáček, Shostakovich, Poulenc, Weill, Stravinsky—older works such as *Idomeneo, La Clemenza di Tito, Rodelinda, Stiffelio, I Lombardi, Semiramide* and new works like *The Ghosts of Versailles, The Voyage, The Great Gatsby, A View from the Bridge, An American Tragedy*—in an amazing variety of production styles.

•

I wouldn't trade it for any other life! And yes, given the opportunity, I would gladly do it again; for the gigantic difficulties and disappointments, the failures and frustrations, are more than offset by the exhilaration, the joy of working with this great company on such great music—and the special pleasure of feeling the audience respond so passionately to all our efforts to try to communicate the composer's and librettist's intentions.

•

The Metropolitan Opera is, on balance, the greatest opera company in the world! (There, I said it!)

# Military Maneuvers, or, Getting Grand Opera on Stage

JOSEPH CLARK

Opera is a most difficult art to capture and record. The moment is everything. One's impressions—often lasting—of that instant when it all clicks, touching off all sorts of Proustian recollections and fleeting sensations, are impossible to put into words or pictures. The visible elements can be recorded on film or video, but can the moment itself be recaptured?

Nancy Ellison's photographs come far closer than anything I have seen to re-creating for me those magical moments in the theater when it all comes together. Yes, there is no music, no live performance, but there is another, wonderfully intangible, element: the ensemble, the group effort. It is the combined effort and contributions of literally hundreds of people, many of whom are behind the scenes, which creates a whole that is far greater than the sum of the parts.

The physical institution of the Met stage is mammoth, with well over one hundred productions in semi-active repertory, almost a thousand forty-foot-long shipping containers filled with scenery, and three storage facilities bulging with props, costumes, armory, hats, wigs, electrical effects, lighting equipment, and so on. One can visit the Old Kingdom tombs of Egypt, the Hanging Gardens of Babylon, the Sahara Desert, the far reaches of the galaxy, Montmartre, or Florence without leaving Manhattan. We are strong

on Rome: the church of Sant'Andrea della Valle, the Farnese Palace, Castel Sant'Angelo, a neoclassical version of the Forum—before and after burning—and the Pantheon are all present. Other settings include humble cottages and grand churches—such as Saint Sulpice—battlefields and mysterious forests, rocky mountain crags and the desolate bayous of Louisiana, and that is just for the first week out. As for the weather, it may be fine with puffy clouds drifting overhead, or stormy with rain, lightning, and thunder, or foggy, or pitch black, or lit by radiant moonlight with stars.

The Met commands one of the largest navies in the world, with vessels from canoes to British men-of-war. Other means of transport include various horse-drawn vehicles—chariots, a hansom cab, or a Wells Fargo coach—several full-fledged motorcars, hot-air balloons, and birds large enough to carry passengers. Every historical and mythological costume period is well represented, from ancient Greece, Troy, and Egypt to uniforms of a distant future when space travel is common. Props may be carried, worn, become weapons, explode, catch fire, disappear, or just remain in place.

An average day sees one rehearsal and performance, with two performances on Saturday, for a staggering fourteen complete opera setups on the stage every week. With a more than thirty-week season and three preparatory weeks, that means roughly 225 operas

to set up and strike in a season, and never the same combination twice, given the demands of a repertory schedule. On an average day, more than a hundred people are busy moving scenery, setting props and ground cloths, focusing lighting, and preparing and dressing the cast—eighty choristers, principals, ballet, and extras, who often require several changes of costume in the course of a performance or rehearsal. On a day with piano alone (no orchestra), the scenery is often sketchy to give the performers just enough to rehearse their staging; for a full orchestra rehearsal, the scenery,

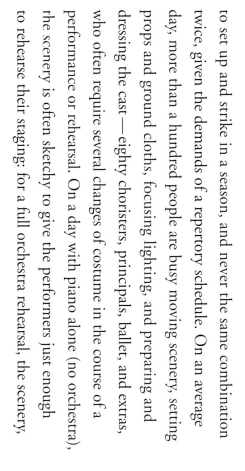

lighting, costumes, wigs, and makeup are prepared just as they would be for a performance. In fact, it is as much a rehearsal for the crew as for the singers, chorus, and orchestra: if things go wrong or need adjustment, this is the time to work them out or improve them before the final dress rehearsal.

The stage crew plays an active part in all rehearsals, not only to properly revive those elements that are their responsibility, but also to improve or repair them, and to choreograph their moves for scene changes, whether visible or invisible to the audience.

Rehearsals also provide the opportunity for new stagehands to learn, if they have not previously worked on a particular opera. Though some information is written down about the thousands of parts that make up a set, or populate it with props, and about how the hundreds of lighting instruments are to be focused, plugged, and cued, there is rarely time in a rehearsal or performance to refer to notes—it has to be largely in everyone's head. The seasoned crew actually knows most standard repertory as well as the performers, and is often caught listening, watching, helping, and encouraging the cast.

Then there are the designers, both guest and resident, who imagine and record their ideas for what that production might look like, along with the armies in the construction, paint, electrical, mechanical, costume, wig, and makeup shops who realize those designs. At every step along the way, from idea to finished product, there is the constant, experienced, talented, imaginative help and guidance of the Met company craftsmen and performers, adding their skills to the mix.

It is when all that thought, instinct, and subtlety combine that great performances—and great performance-moments—occur. And surprisingly, as hard as it is to document, it is that incredible mix that Nancy's photographs have captured over and over again.

# Grand and Glorious

NANCY ELLISON

Although I am devotedly addicted to the grand gesture, it is not all those sobs and gulps of passion torn to tatters that enchant me. Rather it is the profoundly fearless act of commitment and self-determination that these gestures represent. I am moved by the personal risk of existing out on a limb and by the total absence of reticence—something real life simply does not tolerate. Perhaps that is why I attend The Metropolitan Opera, delighting in the glorious music, and happily wallowing in love, loyalty, betrayal, murder, retribution, forgiveness, sacrifice, heroism, and redemption—or, as Paul Theroux has noted, "wallowing in four dimensions!"

Opera at The Met is not for tidy, rigid souls. It is an eloquent, sensuous, delicious mess. Director, and set and costume designer Franco Zeffirelli—one of the world's and the Met's great creative talents, believes opera is "a planet where muses walk together, join hands, and celebrate the arts." Opera derives from the larger-than-life concept first fashioned by the classic Greeks and later expanded by Richard Wagner's dedication to *Gesamtkunstwerk*—a grandiose fusion of the arts, combining singing, acting, storytelling, poetry, painting, dancing, instrumental music, and architecture. From Wagner's innovative use of the darkened theater and his unique design for a partially covered orchestra pit, to today's

interactive, relepresent "meta-medium" (which includes rear-screen video projections, live 3-D holograms, laser light displays, and computer-generated special effects) artists have sought to envelop operagoers in the illusion of an imaginary world.

These talents not only bring their own unique skills to a production, but also convey their knowledge of and inspiration from other art forms. For example, *tenebroso* and *chiaroscuro* lighting techniques, such as those found in the paintings of Georges de la Tour and Caravaggio, abound. The darkened shadows and dramatic beams of light are especially effective on stage. The undulating, curvilinear architecture of Bernini, and the compositions, imagery, and placement of figures found in the work of Rembrandt, Titian, or Rubens, to name a few, can be referenced in productions of *Otello, Tannhäuser,* or *Nabucco* on one night, while on another influences of Balthus, African Senufo masks, Japanese woodcuts, and Kabuki and Noh theater can be seen in Julie Taymor's production of *Die Zauberflöte.*

In unison such massive, demanding egos jump into the great creative abyss, producing wondrously impractical, complicated ideas, visions, and magnificent music which spill out from that huge Met stage onto the audience's awakening senses. Glorious unmiked voices soaring over the orchestra and chorus one moment

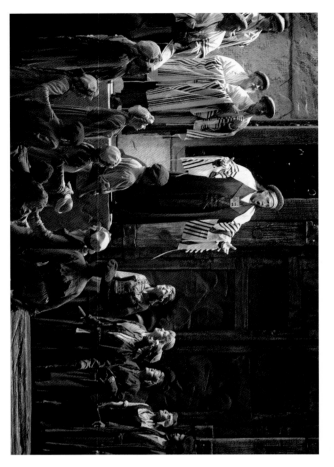

can be modulated to a delicate *fil di voce* in the next. Sets can be anything an art director dreams them to be. Directors can demand horses, chariots, Russian wolfhounds, mechanical birds, or even elephants if needed to dazzle the audience. A three-ring circus? Perhaps, but within this wondrous, voluptuous full-buxom experience, for a moment in time and space, we can sit back and allow truth, love, and beauty to expand our universe and replenish our souls.

Triumph, tragedy, waiting for Gounod . . . opera is as suitable to the retelling of Greek and Teutonic mythology as it is to *verismo*. I am inclined to think it does not really matter what the story is (fairy tale or reality), for as W. H. Auden concluded: "No good opera plot can be sensible, for people don't sing when they are being sensible." Opera requires a suspension of disbelief, an emotional wonder-lust, and a passionate yearning for sound and beauty powerful enough to break through the constraints of everyday life, creating in the process a bit of unconventional spiritual rowdyism.

One master spiritual rowdy, the famous playwright, performer, and lyricist Adolph Green, attended opening night of *Die Fledermaus* in 1998, the Met production for which he and Betty Comden created a new book and English dialogue. To set the scene, this production, unlike any other, begins with the opening bars of *Pagliacci*. Dr. Fledermaus comes from behind the curtain to inform

the maestro that he has started the wrong opera! After this startling beginning, the opera continues on its pun-filled, madcap way. Sitting in one of the grand tier boxes, Green began to sing along with the company—all the parts—causing the black-tie patrons around him to turn in shock. The elfin octogenarian blissfully sang away, with absolutely no awareness of his fellow operagoers, and on key. Who would dare impede that joyous spirit, and who among us at that moment did not want to be as Adolph Green as he?

Luciano Pavarotti, surely one of opera's most beloved spiritual rowdies, once high-fived a nearby supernumerary after landing one of his transcendent high Cs during a performance of *Turandot*. The captivated audience went wild over the sheer joy displayed by the beaming opera singer. "He thinks this is basketball," quipped general manager Joe Volpe in his mischievous *sotto voce*.

Avid opera audiences are always involved, and not all great singing comes from the Met stage. One of the pleasures of a new season is when maestro James Levine conducts the national anthem on opening night and everyone rises to sing. The audience abounds in great voices, but often the voice that is most recognizable above all others is that of the retired, but not retiring, Licia Albanese, the legendary Puccini and Verdi diva who first performed at The Met in 1940.

I experienced many privileged moments while photographing *In Grand Style,* including one that took place during an early piano rehearsal for the premier production of Franco Alfano's *Cyrano de Bergerac.* The supportive stagehands (tenor Charles Anthony calls the Met crew "angels in the outfield") paused to watch the renowned Plácido Domingo. The maestro was wearing a rumpled blue blazer, slacks tucked into swashbuckler boots, and an imposing new nose. He was slowly introducing parts of his costume and character, not only becoming comfortable in the shoes (and nose) of Cyrano but also by these bits and pieces beginning to transform into Cyrano himself. We were witnessing a seminal phase, an actor's *bozzetto,* a sketch in the creative process that would come to mani-

fest itself in his impassioned and noble portrait — a triumph that any stagehand there that day could have predicted.

The most passionate backstage audience, however, was the one Giuseppe Verdi experienced during the first rehearsal of *Nabucco* in 1842. One by one the crew of carpenters at La Scala put down their gear to listen to *"Va, pensiero"* and its plaintive longing for liberty. They listened as if in church, and when the chorus finished, they picked up their tools and in unison began to hammer on stage, creating the most profound ovation Verdi had ever received!

Verdi himself would have been impressed by the love and bittersweet passion, bordering on melancholy, that flowed from the audience to Pavarotti as they paid the incomparable tenor

tribute during his farewell operatic performance. He chose the role of Cavaradossi in Giacomo Puccini's *Tosca* for his finale — his 379th appearance at The Met since his debut in 1968. As the curtain calls began, a banner was unfurled from the dress circle that read, "WE LOVE YOU LUCIANO." The sustained applause, the shouts, the heartbreaking but glorious emotion might well have gone on indefinitely had not Signor Pavarotti waved good-bye for a final time.

All of us who love to attend opera know that we go in anticipation of our grand shared experience, that moment on stage when great voices do indeed soar. In our hearts we say, reach for the stars with every breath you take, for you take us with you.

The Operas

# Der Rosenkavalier

## RICHARD STRAUSS

*The 363rd Metropolitan Opera Performance*
Conductor: Donald Runnicles, Production: Nathaniel Merrill, Set and Costume Designer: Robert O'Hearn, Stage Director: Bruce Donnell,
Octavian: Susan Graham, Princess von Werdenberg: Angela Denoke (debut), Mohammed: Zachary Vail Elkind, The Princess' Major-Domo: John Easterlin,
Baron Ochs auf Lerchenau: Peter Rose, Three Noble Orphans: Anne Nonnemacher, Sandra Bush, Annette Spann, A Noble Widow: Carole Wright,
A Milliner: Patricia Steiner, An Animal Vendor: Kurt Phinney, Valzacchi: Greg Fedderly, An Italian Singer: Matthew Polenzani, A Hairdresser: Sam Meredith,
A Notary: James Courtney, Annina: Wendy White, Leopold: Gregory Lorenz, Lackeys and Waiters: Meredith Derr, Roger Andrews, Marty Singleton,
John Shelhart, Faninal: Håkan Hagegård, Marianne: Claudia Waite, Faninal's Major-Domo: Mark Showalter, Sophie: Laura Aikin,
An Innkeeper: Tony Stevenson, A Police Commissary: Paul Plishka

# La Clemenza di Tito

## WOLFGANG AMADEUS MOZART

*The 30th Metropolitan Opera Performance*

Conductor: James Levine, Production: Jean-Pierre Ponnelle, Set and Costume Designer: Jean-Pierre Ponnelle, Lighting Designer: Gil Wechsler,
Stage Director: Peter McClintock, Tito: Frank Lopardo, Vitellia: Melanie Diener, Servilia: Heidi Grant Murphy, Sesto: Anne Sofie Von Otter,
Annio: Sarah Connolly (debut), Publio: Luca Pisaroni (debut), Berenice: Pi Smith

# Die Zauberflöte

## WOLFGANG AMADEUS MOZART

*The 343rd Metropolitan Opera Performance (Premiere New Production)*

Conductor: James Levine, Production: Julie Taymor (debut), Set Designer: George Tsypin, Costume Designer: Julie Taymor,
Lighting Designer: Donald Holder (debut), Puppet Designers: Julie Taymor and Michael Curry (debut), Choreographer: Mark Dendy (debut),
Tamino: Matthew Polenzani, First Lady: Emily Pulley, Second Lady: Jossie Pérez, Third Lady: Wendy White, Papageno: Rodion Pogossov,
Queen of the Night: Ľubica Vargicová (debut), First Slave: Roger Andrews, Second Slave: Dennis Williams, Third Slave: Glenn Bater,
Monostatos: Volker Vogel (debut), Pamina: Dorothea Röschmann, First Spirit: Aiden Bowman, Second Spirit: Janson Goldberg,
Third Spirit: Lev Pakman, Speaker: Julien Robbins, Sarastro: Kwangchul Youn (debut), First Priest: James Courtney, Second Priest: Bernard Fitch,
Papagena: Anna Christy (debut), First Guard: Garrett Sorenson, Second Guard: Morris Robinson, Flute Solo: Michael Parloff

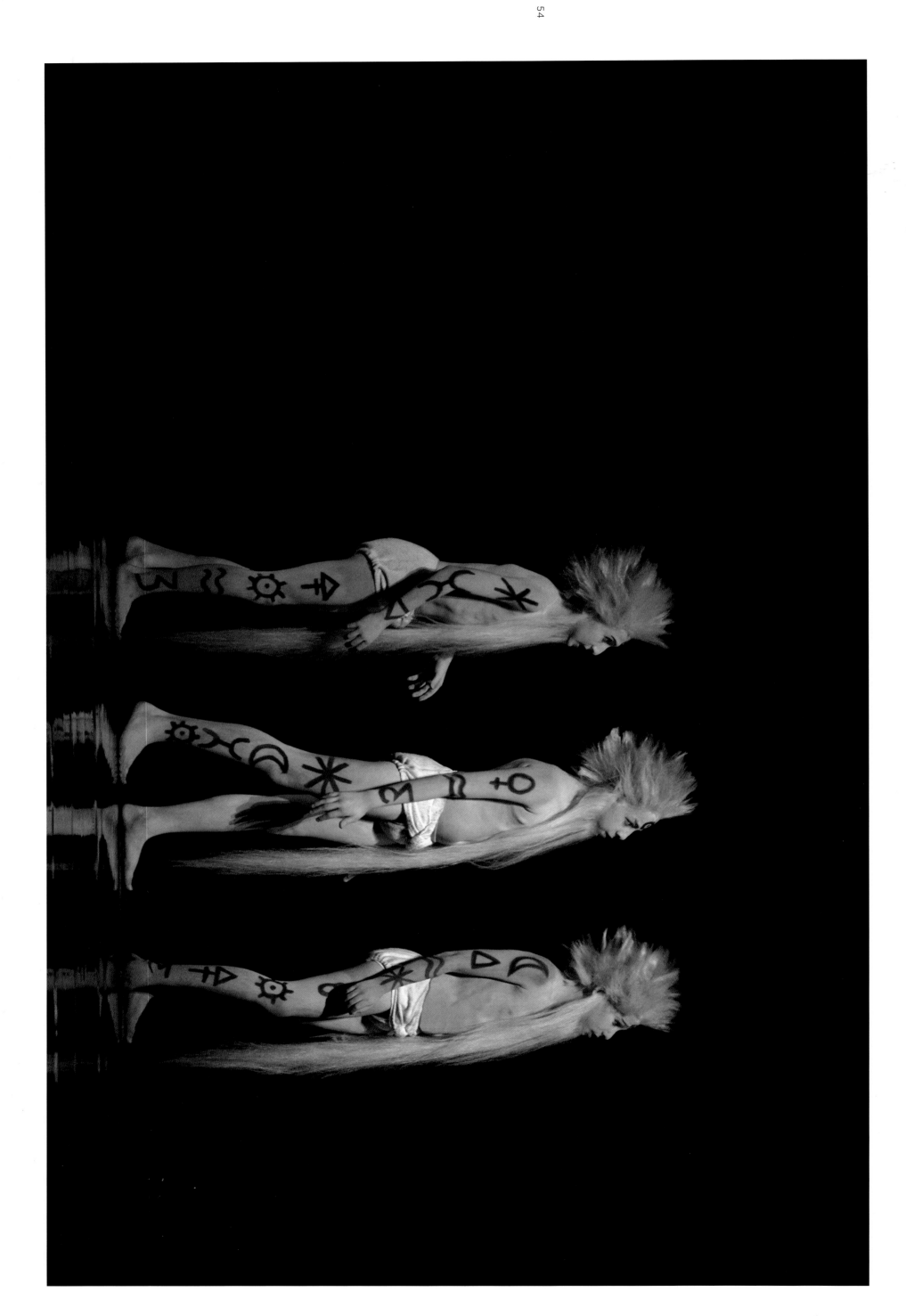

# GIUSEPPE VERDI

*The 107th Metropolitan Opera Performance*
Conductor: Marcello Viotti. Production: Sonja Frisell, Set Designer: Gianni Quaranta. Costume Designer: Dada Saligeri.
Lighting Designer: Gil Wechsler, Choreographer: Rodney Griffin, Stage Director: Zoe Pappas. Ramfis: Kwangchul Youn.
Radames: Franco Farina. Amneris: Dolora Zajick. Aida: Fiorenza Cedolins. The King: Vitalij Kowaljow. A Messenger: Ronald Naldi.
A Priestess: Edyta Kulczak. Amonasro: Juan Pons. Solo Dancers: Christine McMillan, Desiree Sanchez, Jonathan Alsberry.

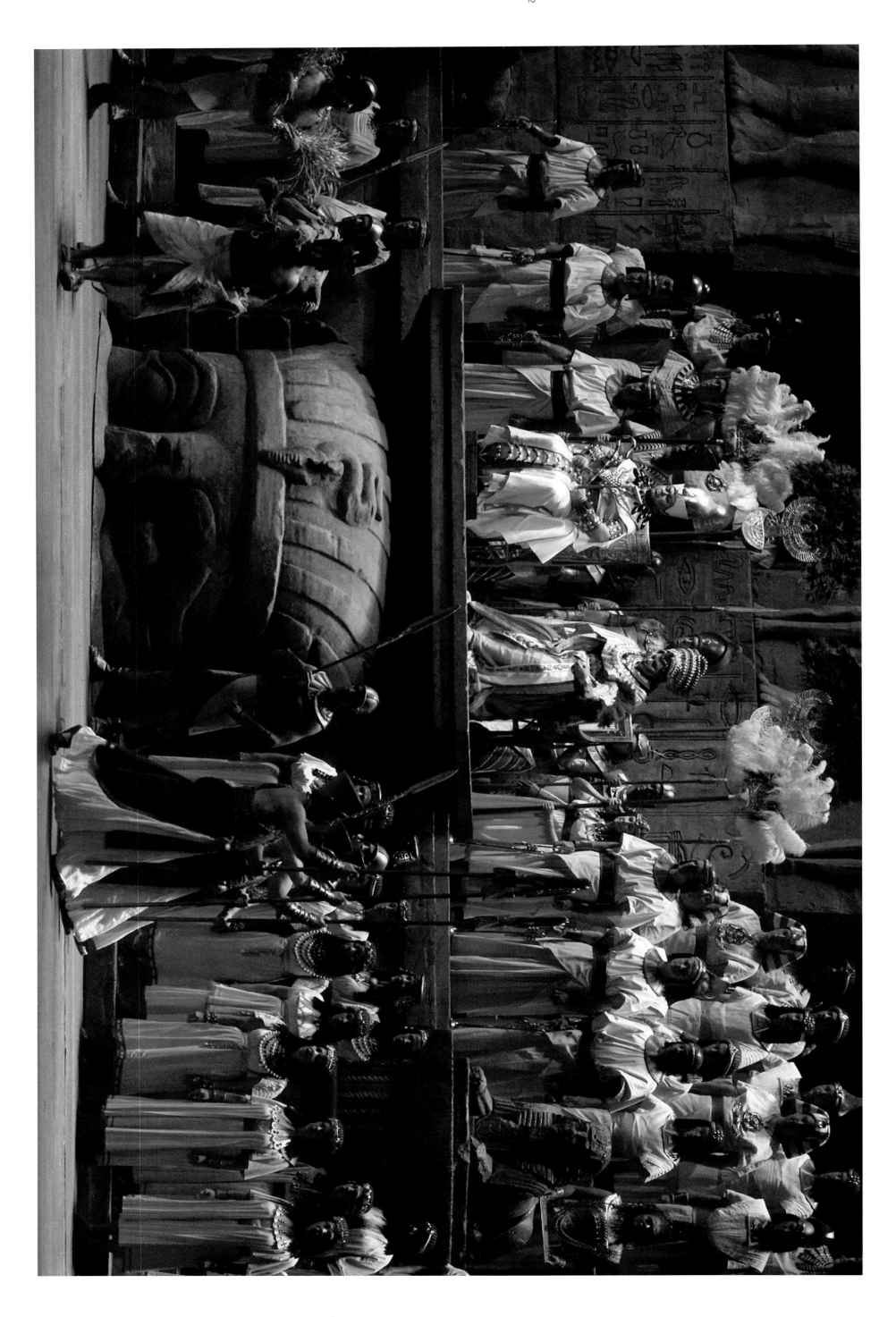

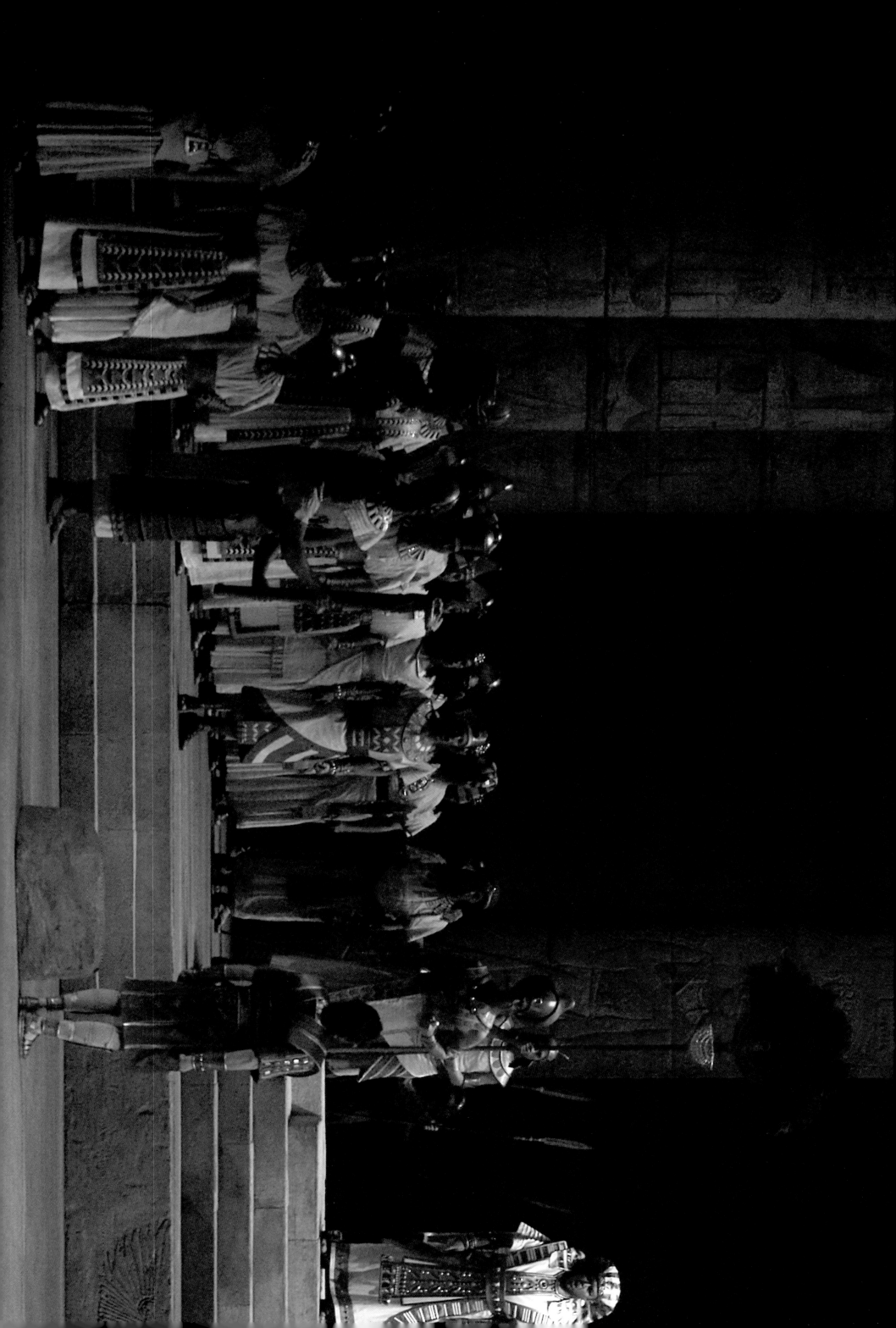

# Pagliacci

## RUGGIERO LEONCAVALLO

*The 689th Metropolitan Opera Performance*
Conductor: Dennis Russell Davies, Production: Franco Zeffirelli, Set and Costume Designer: Franco Zeffirelli,
Stage Director: David Kneuss, Tonio: Juan Pons, Canio: Vladimir Galouzine, Villagers: Daniel C. Smith, Jason Hendrix,
Nedda: Daniela Dessi, Beppe: Philippe Casagner, Silvio: Mariusz Kwiecien

# Nabucco

## GIUSEPPE VERDI

*The 40th Metropolitan Opera Performance*
Conductor: James Levine, Production: Elijah Moshinsky, Set Designer: John Napier, Costume Designer: Andreane Neofitou,
Lighting Designer: Howard Harrison, Stage Director: J Knighten Smit, Abigaille: Maria Guleghina, Fenena: Wendy White,
Ismaele: Gwyn Hughes Jones, Nabucco: Nikolai Putilin, Zaccaria: Paata Burchuladze, Anna: Claudia Waite, Abdallo: Eduardo Valdes,
High Priest of Baal: Julien Robbins

# Cyrano de Bergerac

## FRANCO ALFANO

*Metropolitan Opera Premiere*

Conductor: Marco Armiliato, Production: Francesca Zambello, Set Designer: Peter J. Davison, Costume Designer: Anita Yavich, Lighting Designer: Natasha Katz (debut), Fight Director: Rick Sordelet (debut), Choreographer: Thomas Baird (debut), Le Bret: Julien Robbins, Ragueneau: Roberto de Candia, Christian: Raymond Very, Lignière: Andrew Gangestad, Montfleury: Bernard Fitch, Cyrano: Plácido Domingo, Vicomte de Valvert: Brian Davis, The Duenna: Sheila Nadler, A Cook: Roger Andrews, Lisa: Jennifer Check, A Musketeer: Richard Pearson, Roxane: Sondra Radvanovsky, Carbon: Louis Otey, De Guiche: Anthony Michaels-Moore, Sentinels: David Frye, Gregory Cross, The Spanish Official: Brian Davis, A Lay Sister: Jennifer Check, Sister Marta: Diane Elias

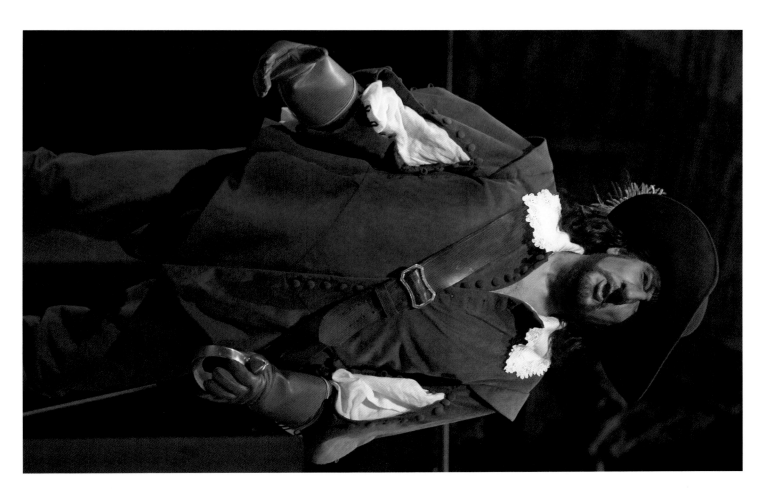

# La Bohème

## GIACOMO PUCCINI

*The 1,152nd Metropolitan Opera Performance*

Conductor: Daniel Oren, Production: Franco Zeffirelli, Set Designer: Franco Zeffirelli, Costume Designer: Peter J. Hall,
Lighting Designer: Gil Wechsler, Stage Director: J. Knighten Smit, Marcello: Peter Mattei, Rodolfo: Marcelo Álvarez,
Colline: Evgenij Nikitin, Schaunard: Patrick Carfizzi, Benoit: Paul Plishka, Mimì: Ruth Ann Swenson, Parpignol: Meredith Derr,
Alcindoro: Paul Plishka, Musetta: Ainhoa Arteta, Customhouse Sergeant: Joseph Pariso, Customhouse Officer: Glenn Bater

# Samson et Dalila

## CAMILLE SAINT-SAËNS

*The 210th Metropolitan Opera Performance*

Conductor: Bertrand de Billy; Production: Elijah Moshinsky, Set and Costume Designer: Richard Hudson,
Lighting Designer: Duane Schuler, Choreographer: Graeme Murphy; Stage Director: Peter McClintock, Samson: José Cura,
Abimélech: James Courtney; The High Priest: Jean-Philippe LaFont, First Philistine: Bernard Fitch, Second Philistine:
Richard Hobson, A Philistine Messenger: Tony Stevenson, An Old Hebrew: Vitalij Kowaljow, Dalila: Denyce Graves

# I Vespri Siciliani

GIUSEPPE VERDI

*The 38th Metropolitan Opera Performance*
Conductor: Frédéric Chaslin, Production: John Dexter, Set Designer: Josef Svoboda, Costume Designer: Jan Skalicky;
Associate Designer: David Reppa, Lighting Director: Wayne Chouinard, Choreographer: Joseph Fritz, Stage Director: Peter McClintock,
Tebaldo: Eduardo Valdes, Roberto: Sebastian Catana, Di Bethune: Peter Volpe, Vaudemont: Andrew Gangestad, Manfredo: Tony Stevenson,
Elena: Sondra Radvanovsky, Danieli: Ronald Naldi, Ninetta: Jane Bunnell, Guido di Monforte: Leo Nucci, Arrigo: Francisco Casanova,
Giovanni da Procida: Samuel Ramey

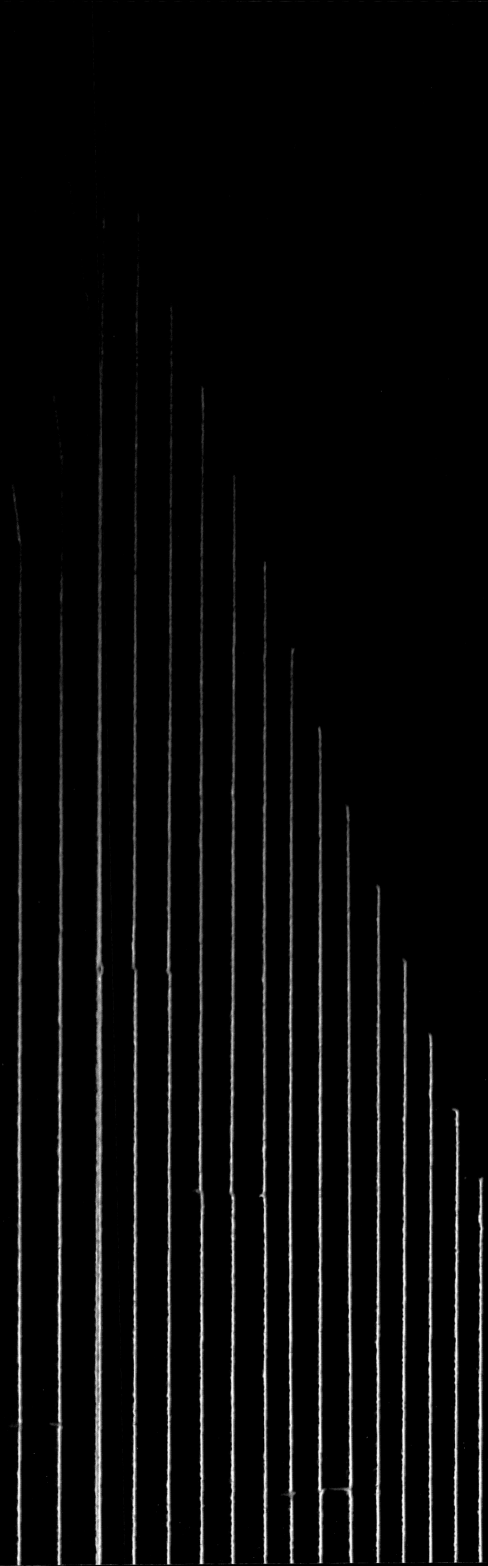

# Carmen

## GEORGES BIZET

*The 921st Metropolitan Opera Performance*

Conductor: Plácido Domingo. Production: Franco Zeffirelli. Set Designer: Franco Zeffirelli. Costume Designer: Anna Anni.
Lighting Designer: Duane Schuler. Choreographer: Maria Benitez. Stage Director: Peter McClintock. Morales: Brian Davis. Micaela:
Hei-Kyung Hong. Don José: Eduardo Villa. Zuniga: James Courtney. Carmen: Irina Mishura. Frasquita: Jennifer Welch-Babidge.
Mercédès: Sandra Piques Eddy. Escamillo: Ildar Abdrazakov. Le Dancaïre: Jeff Mattsey. Le Remendado: Eduardo Valdes

# Le Nozze di Figaro

### WOLFGANG AMADEUS MOZART

*The 415th Metropolitan Opera Performance*
Conductor: James Levine, Production: Jonathan Miller, Set Designer: Peter Davison, Costume Designer: James Acheson,
Lighting Designer: Mark McCullough, Stage Director: Robin Guarino, Choreographer: Terry John Bates, Figaro: John Relyea,
Susanna: Andrea Rost, Don Bartolo: Paul Plishka, Marcellina: Jane Bunnell, Cherubino: Jossie Pérez, Count Almaviva: Mariusz Kwiecien,
Don Basilio: Michel Sénéchal, Countess Almaviva: Janice Watson, Antonio: Patrick Carfizzi, Don Curzio: Tony Stevenson,
Barbarina: Yvonne Gonzales Redman, Bridesmaids: Anita Johnson, Edyta Kulczak

# Otello

## GIUSEPPE VERDI

*The 306th Metropolitan Opera Performance (This performance was dedicated to the memory of Renata Tebaldi)*
Conductor: James Levine, Production: Elijah Moshinsky, Set Designer: Michael Yeargan, Costume Designer: Peter J. Hall,
Lighting Designer: Duane Schuler, Choreographer: Eleanor Fazan, Stage Director: Sharon Thomas, Montano: Charles Taylor,
Cassio: Garrett Sorenson, Iago: Carlo Guelfi, Roderigo: Bernard Fitch, Otello: Ben Heppner, Desdemona: Barbara Frittoli,
Emilia: Jane Bunnell, A Herald: Brian Davis, Lodovico: Vitalij Kowaljow

# Tannhäuser

## RICHARD WAGNER

*The 463rd Metropolitan Opera Performance*

Conductor: Mark Elder, Production: Otto Schenk, Set Designer: Günther Schneider-Siemssen, Costume Designer: Patricia Zipprodt,

Lighting Designer: Gil Wechsler, Choreographer: Norbert Vesak, Stage Director: Stephen Pickover, Venus: Michelle DeYoung,

Tannhäuser: Peter Seiffert (debut), A Young Shepherd: Jason Goldberg, Hermann: Kwangchul Youn, Walter von der Vogelweide: John Horton Murray,

Biterolf: Charles Taylor, Wolfram von Eschenbach: Thomas Hampson, Heinrich der Schreiber: Roy Cornelius Smith, Reinmar von Zweter: Morris Robinson,

Elisabeth: Deborah Voigt, Pages: Aiden Bowman, Jesse Dembo, Garrett Eucker, Jason Goldberg, Chris Kelly, Josh Kohane, Ryan Mandelbaum,

Dmitri Williams, Three Graces: Sarah Weber Gallo, Jenny Sandler, Rachel Schuette

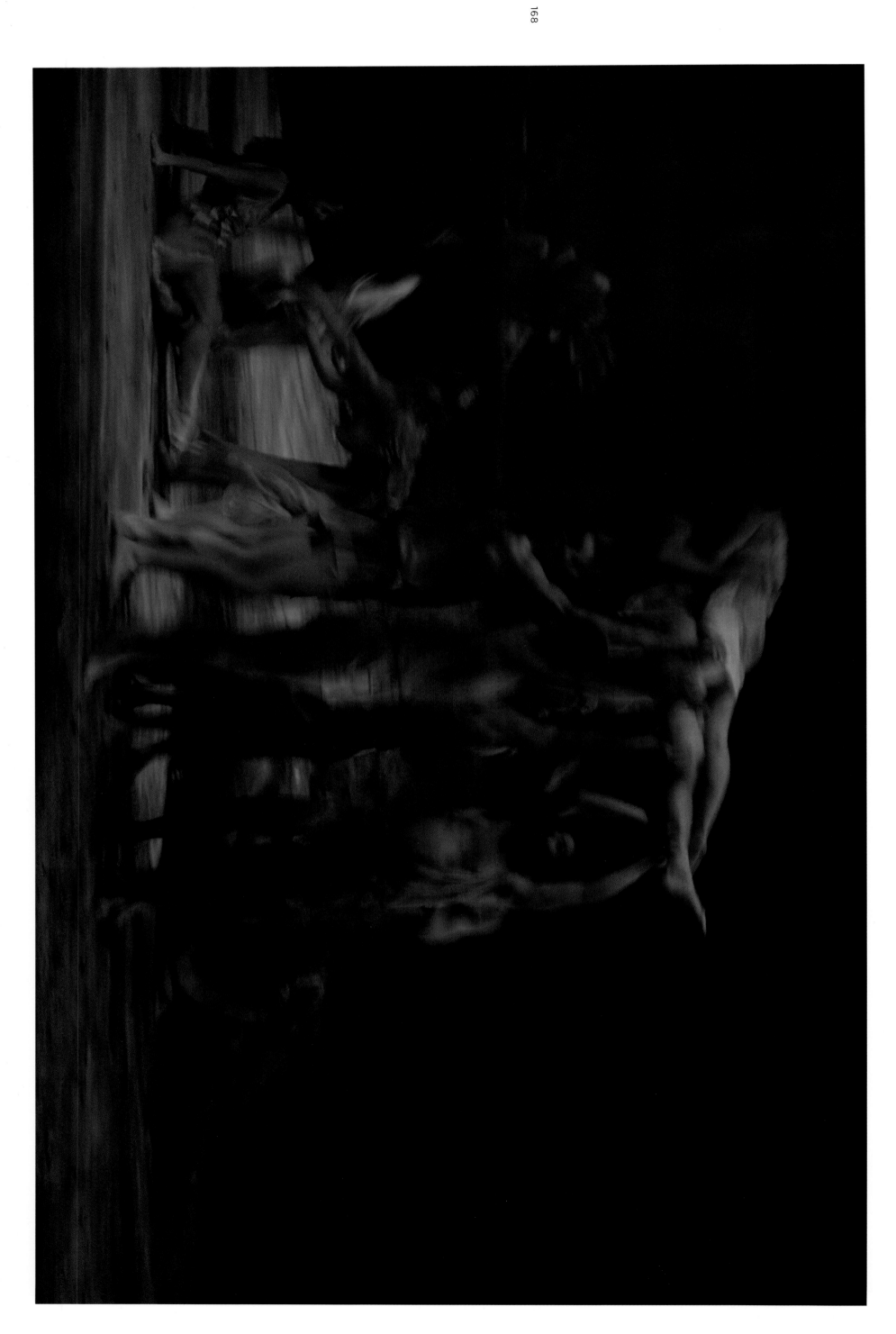

# Rodelinda

GEORGE FRIDERIC HANDEL

*The 8th Metropolitan Opera Performance*
Conductor: Harry Bicket, Production: Stephen Wadsworth, Set Designer: Thomas Lynch, Costume Designer: Martin Pakledinaz,
Lighting Director: Peter Kaczorowski, Rodelinda: Renée Fleming, Grimoaldo: Kobie van Rensburg, Garibaldo: John Relyea,
Eduige: Stephanie Blythe, Bertarido: David Daniels, Unulfo: Bejun Mehta, Flavio: Zachary Vail Elkind

# Salome

## RICHARD STRAUSS

*The 147th Metropolitan Opera Performance*

Conductor: Valery Gergiev; Production: Jürgen Flimm, Set and Costume Designer: Santo Loquasto, Lighting Designer: James F. Ingalls, Choreographer: Doug Varone; Narraboth: Matthew Polenzani, The Page: Katharine Goeldner, First Soldier: Peter Volpe, Second Soldier: Richard Bernstein, Jochanaan: Bryn Terfel, A Cappadocian: Andrew Gangestad, Salome: Karita Mattila, A Slave: Vanessa Cariddi, Herod: Siegfried Jerusalem, Herodias: Larissa Diadkova, First Jew: Allan Glassman, Second Jew: Roy Cornelius Smith, Third Jew: Adam Klein, Fourth Jew: John Easterlin, Fifth Jew: LeRoy Lehr, First Nazarene: Morris Robinson, Second Nazarene: Charles Edwin Taylor

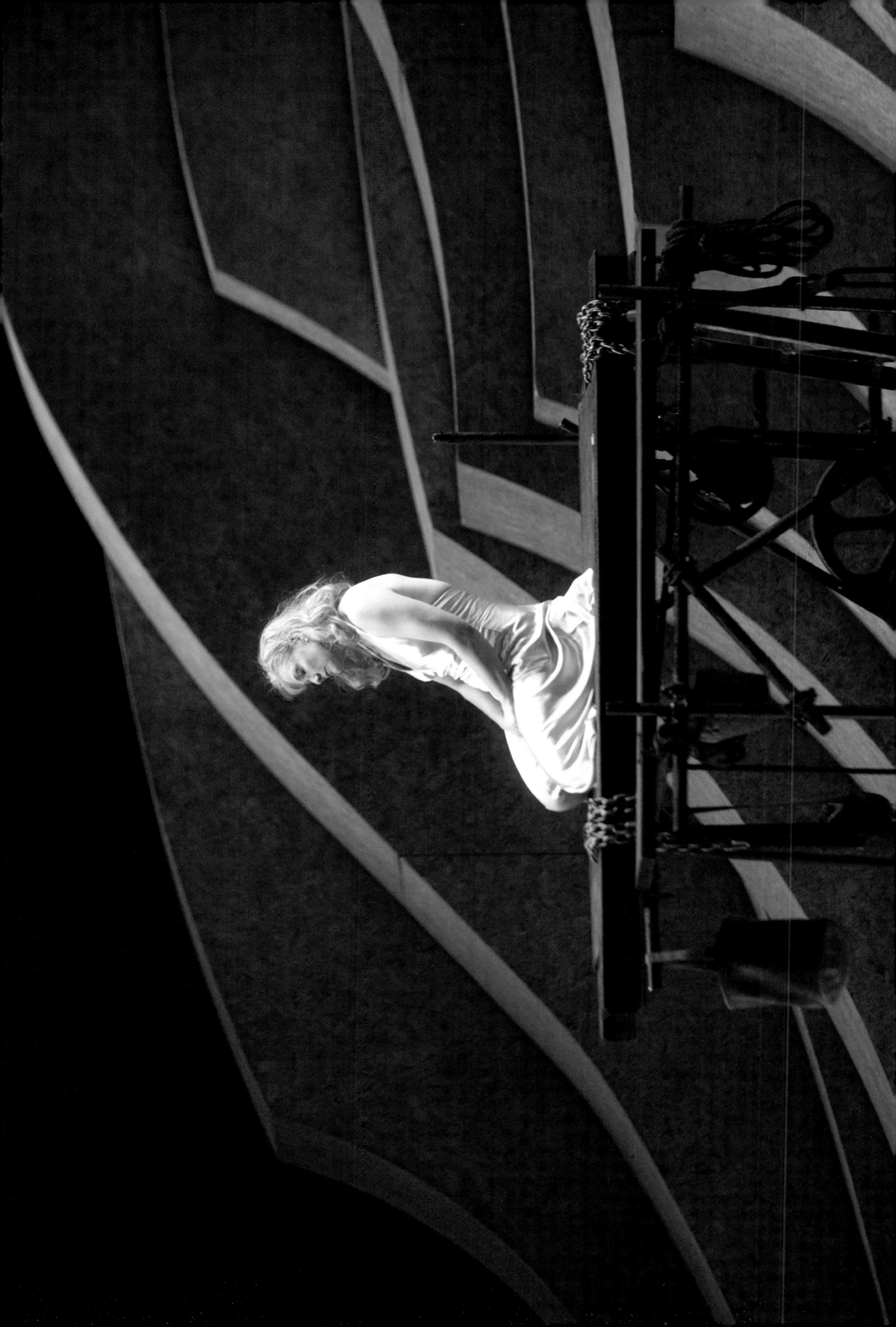

# Un Ballo in Maschera

## GIUSEPPE VERDI

*The 271st Metropolitan Opera Performance*

Conductor: James Conlon, Production: Piero Faggioni, Set and Costume Designer: Piero Faggioni, Lighting Designer: Piero Faggioni,
Stage Director: Laurie Feldman, Amelia: Deborah Voigt, Oscar: Lyubov Petrova, Ulrica: Marianne Cornetti, Riccardo: Marcello Giordani,
Renato: Carlos Alvarez, Silvano: Brian Davis, Sam: Hao Jiang Tian, Tom: Paul Plishka, Judge: Bernard Fitch, Servant: Tony Stevenson,
Solo Dancers: Linda Gelinas, Griff Braun, Sam Meredith

# Faust

## CHARLES GOUNOD

*The 714th Metropolitan Opera Performance*
Conductor: James Levine, Production: Andrei Serban, Set and Costume Designer: Santo Loquasto, Lighting Designer: Duane Schuler,
Choreographer: Nikolaus Wolcz, Faust: Roberto Alagna, Méphistophélès: René Pape, Wagner: Patrick Carfizzi, Valentin: Dmitri Hvorostovsky,
Siébel: Kristine Jepson, Marguerite: Soile Isokoski, Marthe: Jane Bunnell

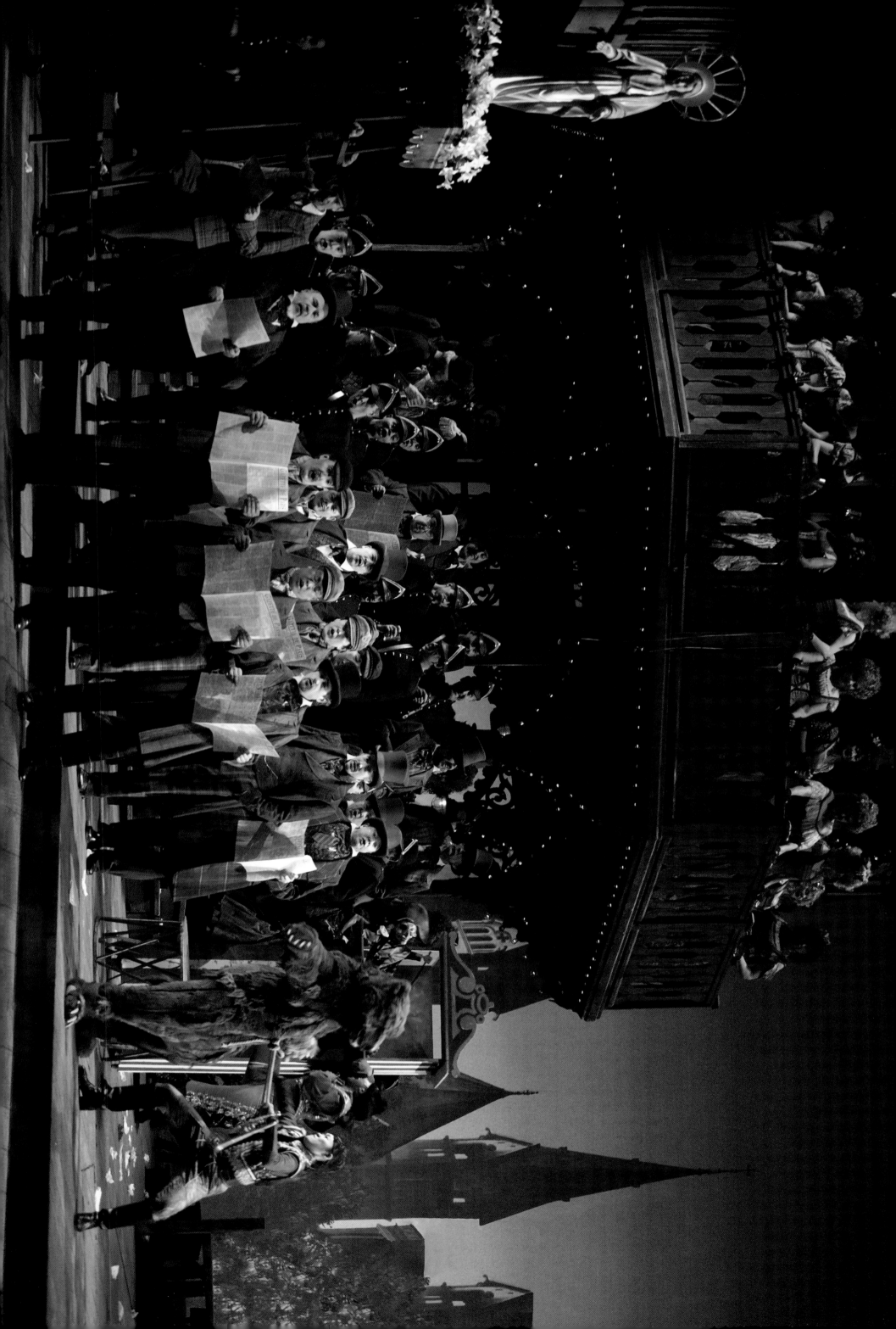

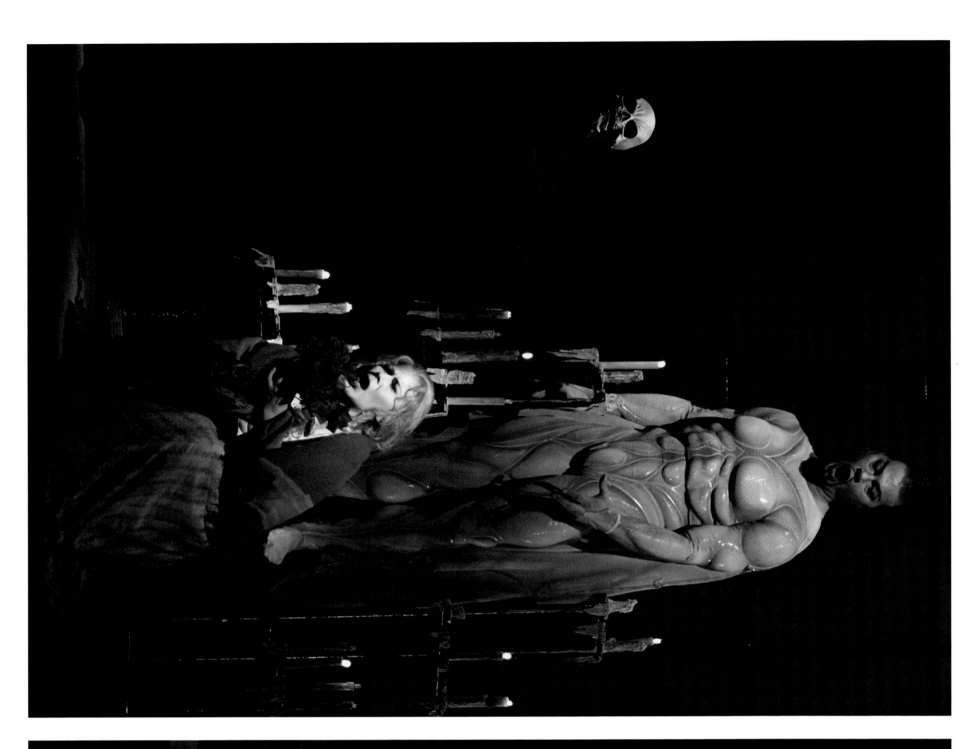

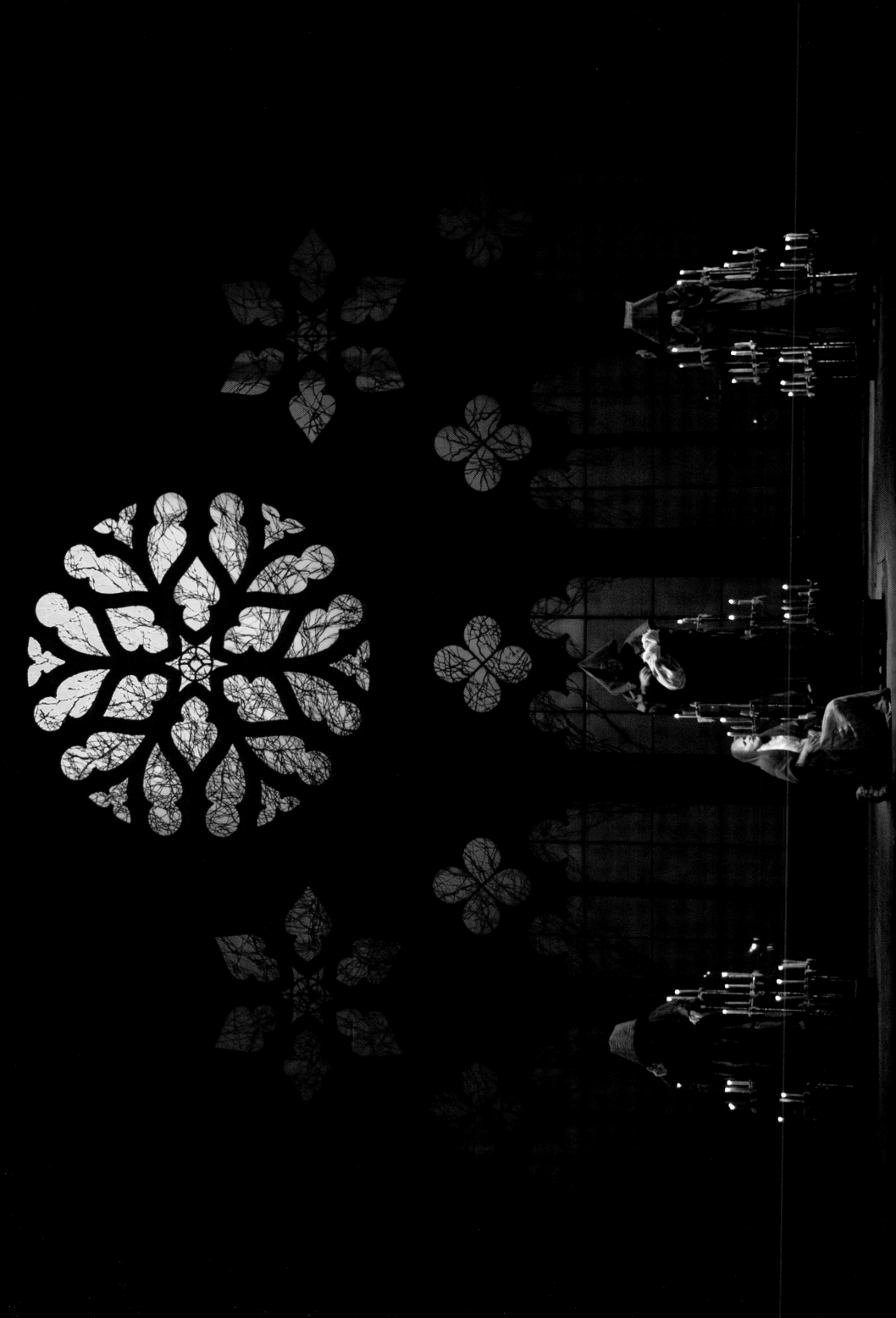

# Turandot

## GIACOMO PUCCINI

*The 246th Metropolitan Opera Performance*

Conductor: Bertrand de Billy, Production: Franco Zeffirelli, Set Designer: Franco Zeffirelli, Costume Designers: Anna Anni, Dada Saligeri,
Lighting Designer: Gil Wechsler, Choreographer: Chiang Ching, Stage Director: David Kneuss, Turandot: Andrea Gruber, Liù: Krassimira Stoyanova,
Calàf: Johan Botha, Timur: Hao Jiang Tian, Ping: Haijing Fu, Pang: Tony Stevenson, Pong: Eduardo Valdes, Emperor: Charles Anthony,
Mandarin: James Courtney, Prince of Persia: Sasha Semin, Executioner: Jason Kuschner, Handmaidens: Lynn Taylor, April Haines, Masks: José Bercero,
Sam Meredith, Andrew Robinson, Temptresses: Sarah Weber Gallo, Linda Gelinas, Annemarie Lucania, Rachel Schuette

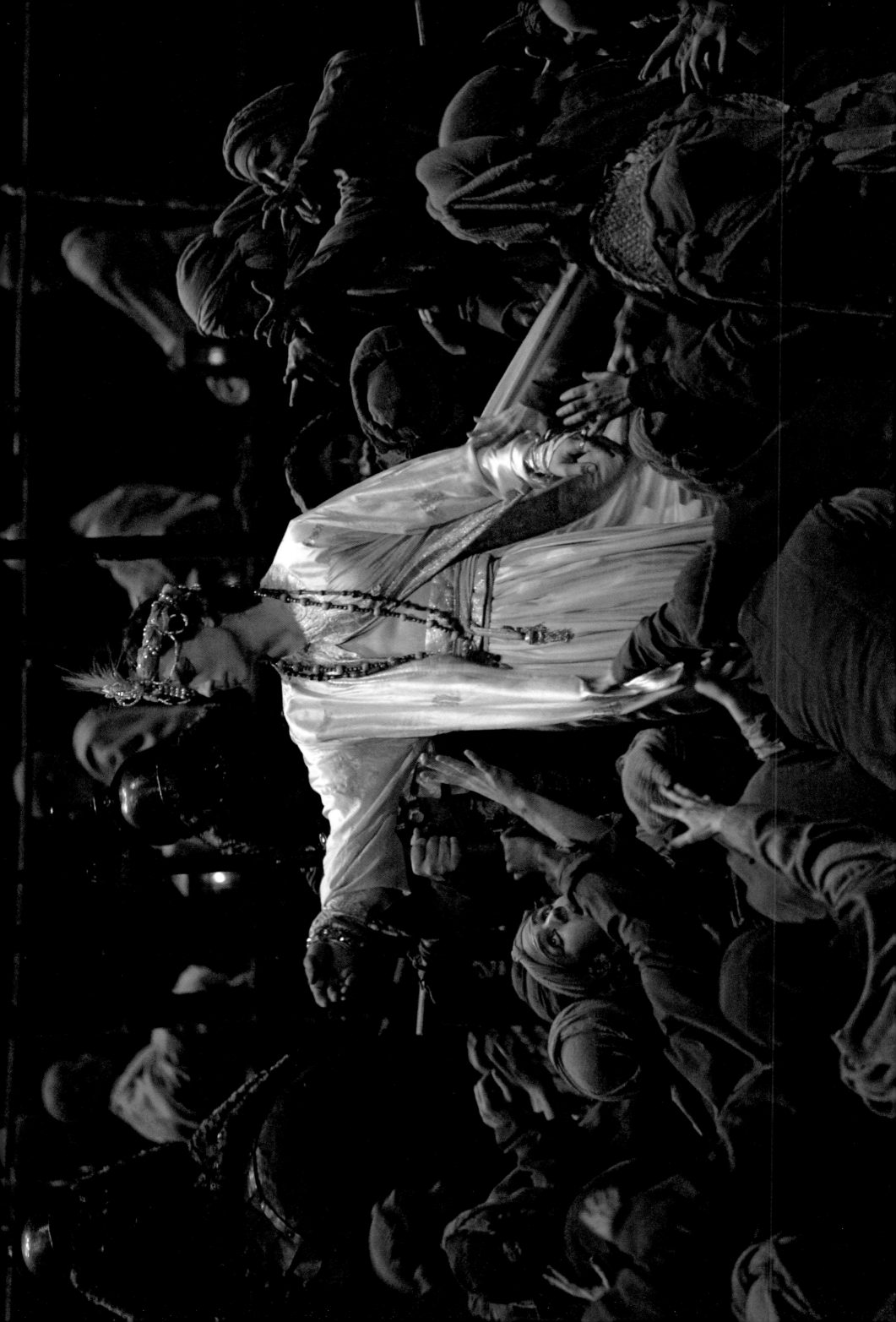

# Tosca

## GIACOMO PUCCINI

The 856th Metropolitan Opera Performance (This evening marks Luciano Pavarotti's farewell to The Metropolitan Opera in a staged performance.)

Conductor: James Levine. Production: Franco Zeffirelli. Set Designer: Franco Zeffirelli. Costume Designer: Peter J. Hall. Stage Director: Sharon Thomas. Angelotti: James Courtney. Sacristan: Paul Plishka. Cavaradossi: Luciano Pavarotti. Tosca: Carol Vaness. Scarpia: Samuel Ramey. Spoletta: Charles Anthony. Sciarrone: Richard Vernon. Shepherd: Sara Appleton. Jailer: Leroy Lehr

WE L♡VE YOU LUCIANO

# Acknowledgments

When I asked Joseph Volpe if I could do a book on The Met and Opera, he not only opened the physical doors of this incredible institution but also led me to its heart and soul. For fourteen months I joyously felt part of its creative collective. Allowed to photograph at will, and with the kindness and support of everyone under his leadership, I have collected images that far exceed the generous space provided by Rizzoli. I thank you, Joe, from the depths of my heart. Maestro James Levine offered me a glimpse into his musical process, and I felt honored to have had the opportunity to hear Jimmy, eyes often closed in rapt concentration, rehearse the great Met Orchestra. Joseph Clark, technical master of production, took me under his wing during rehearsals, giving me an indispensable overview. All three graciously agreed to contribute text for *In Grand Style*, which indeed makes this volume both unique and definitive. To you three brilliant men, my thanks are infinite.

To everyone in Met publicity: François Giuliani, Peter Clark, Charles Sheek, Jonathan Tichler, and Jennifer Carle, I thank you. Peter Clark was a guiding presence throughout both the principal photography and the post-production sessions for *In Grand Style*. If there was a problem, a request, or a question, Peter was the one to call. Always gracious, he made all things possible. Thank you.

To Robert Tuggle, archives director, and to everyone in the executive offices—Ann Coughlin, Mary Pat Fortier, and Ilana Frankel—I did so appreciate your help. To Sylvia Nolan, resident costume designer, Lesley Weston, head of the Met's Costume Shop, and Vicki Tanner, assistant wardrobe supervisor. Thank you for your gracious assistance. To Raymond Hughes, the Met chorus master, and Elena Doria and Bob Diamond of the Met's Children's Chorus, thank you for allowing me to photograph your rehearsals.

Photographers are seldom allowed to be in the midst of the backstage action during performances and rehearsals. I wish I could present the magnitude of activity that goes on, and I wish every reader could have been by my side—especially during Act Two of *Aida*, with its grand procession. I have never had so much fun. My thanks to assistant technical director John Sellars, production stage manager Tom Connell, stage manager Gary Dietrich, their staff, and everyone backstage who pointed out great photo ops (such as when supernumeraries rushed to change from warrior costumes to slave attire) and who literally watched my back during scene changes. I felt the whole company wanted me to succeed, and if I may have been in their way, their kindness prevented them from making me self-conscious. My deepest respect and gratitude; you all are truly "angels in the outfield."

"It must be Rizzoli!" enthused publisher Charles Miers, and so it was—an Italian publishing house doing our book on opera—a match indeed. *Mille grazie* to Charles, with respect, appreciation, and friendship. To my buddy, my editor Sandy Gilbert, how happy I am to be working with you—you are the best. Ellen Nidy, managing editor, and Anet Sirna-Bruder, production director, both brought not only their professional expertise but also their love of opera to this project. Thank you.

To the talented artists at Anthony McCall Associates, Mark Nelson, design director, and David Zaza, studio director, please know how truly appreciative I am. Our collaboration together on *In Grand Style* has been a pleasure and a privilege.

To Helen Cantu and Walter Murdock, many thanks for your technical expertise and assistance. Helen, special thanks for keeping me on track.

I lovingly thank my friends who acted as sounding boards for me, and whose opinions I trust and respect: Rosabeth Kanter, Alan Dershowitz, and Paul Theroux.

. . . And to the incomparable Luciano Pavarotti, *grazie infinite*. Your heavenly voice ever rings in our hearts.

Photographs accompanying essays:
Pages 6 *Le Nozze di Figaro* rehearsal; 10 *Die Zauberflöte*;
12 Striking the set for *Cyrano de Bergerac*; 14-15 *Cyrano de Bergerac*
rehearsal; 16 (left) *Aida* and (right) costume change; 18 (top) Rembrandt,
*Christ Preaching*, etching, c.1656, Private Collection, (bottom) Samuel
Ramey as Zaccaria in *Nabucco*; 19 Plácido Domingo in rehearsal (left)
and in performance (right) of *Cyrano de Bergerac*; 22-23 *Aida*, Act II,
Triumphal Scene; Front cover Luciano Pavarotti as Cavaradossi and
Carol Vaness as Tosca in *Tosca*; Back cover Andrea Gruber as Turandot
and Johan Botha as Calàf in *Turandot*.

First published in the United States of America in 2006
by Rizzoli International Publications, Inc.
300 Park Avenue South
New York, New York 10010
www.rizzoliusa.com

Copyright © 2005 Rizzoli International Publications, Inc.
Photographs copyright © 2005 Nancy Ellison

Project Editor: Sandra Gilbert
Photo Editors: Mark Nelson and Nancy Ellison
Design: Anthony McCall Associates

ISBN-10: 0-8478-2799-2
ISBN-13: 978-0-8478-2799-2
Library of Congress Catalog Control Number: 2005931843
2005 2006 2007 2008 / 10 9 8 7 6 5 4 3 2 1

Printed in China